Lieutenant
Desmond L.S. Arthur
RFC

The
Life and Death
of an
Aviator

Barry Dominic Graham

This is a work of historical non-fiction.

Copyright © 2020 by Barry Dominic Graham

The moral right of Barry Dominic Graham
to be identified as the author and creator of this work
has been asserted by him
in accordance with the Copyrights, Designs and Patents Act 1988

Registered with

No. 284672969

ISBN: 9798676139544

FIRST EDITION

Cover art, interior design, editing and layout by
Barry Dominic Graham

THIS BOOK IS PROFOUNDLY DEDICATED
TO THE MEMORY OF
LIEUTENANT DESMOND L.S. ARTHUR RFC
… AND ALL THE OTHER VALIANT FALLEN HEROES OF AVIATION.

"NE OBLIVISCAMUR"
(LEST WE FORGET)

"Once you have tasted flight,
you will forever walk the earth with your eyes turned skywards."

Leonardo da Vinci
Italian polymath of the High Renaissance
1452 ~ 1519

Foreward

As the Chairman of the Montrose Air Station Heritage Centre, it is always rewarding to learn that the story of another one of our daring young men 'in his flying machine' is to be brought back to life within books such as this one.

Lt. Desmond Arthur was a young man of his time who dared to take up the challenge of conquering the newly discovered thrill of flight.

Alas, his time was cut short as with many young pilots who were involved in flying duties with the Royal Flying Corps in the pre-World War One period.

Desmond is often referred to affectionately by members of the museum staff when the occasional piece of paper or sets of keys go missing and turn up mysteriously elsewhere.

Some believe that Desmond still visits us and we have gained a tremendous amount of media coverage about his alleged hauntings, whether it is real or not... we still remain grateful for his memory and long lasting assistance.

Time as ever is constantly wearing away the memory of those who have gone before us but, knowing the author as well as I do, I am convinced that Barry will apply his usual high standard of sensitivity and will look to reveal as much of the memory of Desmond, past and present, as his considerable talents will lead him to discover.

I have no doubt that this book will be well read, and who knows... perhaps Desmond will read the copy that will be left for him at the museum every evening.

To Lt. Desmond L.S. Arthur RFC... I say thank you for your past, present and future in helping to support the Montrose Air Station Heritage Centre and Museum.

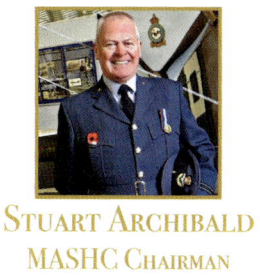

Stuart Archibald
MASHC Chairman

Lt. Desmond Phelps Pery Lucius Studdert Arthur RFC

Preface

It should be said that the character and history of Lt. Desmond L. S. Arthur have a certain charm which has engaged the interest of most, if not all, of those who ever knew anything about them.

Aside from his intrepid and romantic nature, he was well known for his "unassuming manner, optimism and unfailing good Spirit".

Unfortunately there is very little information available regarding the life and times of Lt. Arthur, but I have endeavoured to garner as much as possible for this biography… brief as it is.

My only hope is that I may ultimately serve his memory well and true.

What information now exists is primarily due to the generosity and efforts of certain 'Arthur' and 'Willcox' family descendants… subsequently being preserved and nurtured by the tireless and dedicated volunteers who staff and manage the wonderful 'Montrose Air Station Heritage Centre'.

My sole purpose is merely to help keep alive the memory of someone whom I have no doubt whatsoever deserves to be remembered… as do so many others.

It has been suggested in the past that Desmond Arthur was simply a 'daredevil' who willingly courted death… but I personally would assert the opposite. I believe that people such as he are highly competent and trained individuals who possess a profound knowledge of themselves, being intrinsically driven to overcome their inherent fears by exploring their potential and pushing their limits ever further… resulting in an affirmation of life… rather than the wish and pursuit of death.

Barry D. Graham
Author

```
                                                    233
ARTHUR, Desmond Lucius.
                 ———

Born   31st March, 1884, at Glanomera, Co.Clare
Nationality   British
Rank or Profession   Lieut., Army
Certificate taken on   Bristol Monoplane
At   Brooklands
Date   18th June, 1912
Deceased   27th May, 1913
```

LT. ARTHUR'S 'ROYAL AERO CLUB' FLYING CERTIFICATE NO.233
(OBTAINED AT BROOKLANDS AVIATION GROUND, WEYBRIDGE, SURREY, ENGLAND)

Portrait of an Aviator

II

INTRODUCTION

Lieutenant Desmond L.S. Arthur was an Irish aviator in No.2 Squadron of the Royal Flying Corps.

In the early morning of Tuesday, 27th of May, 1913... while flying over the Scottish North-East coastal town of Montrose, during a routine training flight from Upper Dysart to Lunan Bay, the right wing of his B.E.2 biplane No. 205 suddenly collapsed due to a broken spar, which had hitherto remained unseen... as it had been concealed under the plane's fabric... possibly on purpose.

Lt. Arthur was the first Irishman to be killed in an aircraft accident.

He was buried with full military honours in Sleepyhillock Cemetery of Montrose, being the first pilot to be interred there.

His earthly life was one of courage, romance and tragedy... which many avow... has never ended!

Impelle Obstantia
"Thrust aside obstacles"

14

Contents

Foreward..................................7

Preface...................................9

Introduction..............................13

The History...............................17

Roll of Honour............................47

Acknowledgements..........................61

Bibliography..............................63

About the Author..........................65

Per Ardua ad Astra
"Through Adversity to the Stars"

DESMOND PHELPS PERY LUCIUS STUDDERT ARTHUR WAS BORN ON THE 31ST OF MARCH IN 1884… INTO AN ILLUSTRIOUS UPPER-CLASS IRISH FAMILY LIVING IN GLENOMERA HOUSE (OR GLANOMERA) AT BALLYQUIN, O'BRIENSBRIDGE IN COUNTY CLARE.

HE WAS THE SECOND SON OF THOMAS LUCIUS JERVIS ARTHUR (C.1847-1888) AND CONSTANCE HELEN STUDDERT (C.1859-1902), WHO WAS THE DAUGHTER OF WILLIAM STEELE STUDDERT AND CONSTANCE MASSY OF CLONBOY, COUNTY CLARE.

THE ARTHURS WERE MAJOR LANDOWNERS IN CLARE, OWNING 10,534 ACRES OF LAND. THEY ARE STATED TO HAVE BEEN ORIGINALLY 'ARTUREIGHS'… AND TO DERIVE THEIR DESCENT FROM A COMMON ANCESTOR WITH THE O'BRIENS… NAMELY CORMAC CAS, KING OF MUNSTER (AN HISTORICAL KING OF MUNSTER IN THE LATE 7TH CENTURY AND LEGENDARY ANCESTOR OF SUCH DÁL CAIS (OR DÁL GCAIS) FAMILIES AS THE O'BRIENS AND THE MCNAMARAS. HE WAS A GRANDSON OF EÓGAN MÓR (MUG NUADAT) AND A SON OF AILILL AULOMM, AND THUS SOMETIMES BEARS THE PATRONYMIC MAC AILILLA. SLAIN BY THE INVADING DÉISI AT CARN FERADAIG NEAR THE PRESENT CITY OF LIMERICK, AD 713).

THE NAME WAS ANGLICISED, IN COMMON WITH MANY OTHERS, UPON THE INVASION OF IRELAND BY HENRY II, WHO IS STATED TO HAVE CONFERRED HONOURS AND GRANTS OF LAND ON A ROYALIST OF THAT NAME IN 1178.

IN THE RECORDS OF LIMERICK, THE NAME OF ARTHUR FREQUENTLY OCCURS FROM THE EARLIEST PERIOD DOWN TO THE TIME OF CHARLES I, WHEN THE FAMILY ESTATES IN COUNTY LIMERICK WERE CONFISCATED BY OLIVER CROMWELL FOR SUPPORTING THE ROYALIST CAUSE. THE ARTHURS THEN RELOCATED TO COUNTY CLARE… AND BECAME SEATED AT GLENOMERA.

Glenomera House was an early 18th century three-storey structure with projecting wings, which may possibly represent the original building. The house is said to have burned down in 1905... and was not rebuilt.

Glenomera House
(Ballyquin, County Clare, Ireland)

Thomas L. J. Arthur was the eldest son of Reverend Lucius Arthur (c.1810-1887) and Caroline Elizabeth Jervis (c.1812-1869), daughter of John Heycock Jervis of Moseley, Birmingham, Warwickshire... and was born on the 30th of June in 1847. He was a Lieutenant in the Durham Fusiliers and Captain in the 6th Rifle Volunteers... being also the 'Justice of the Peace' for County Clare. He married Constance Helen Studdert on the 28th of April in 1881.

When Thomas Smith Arthur (c.1806-1884), who had suffered from mental illness (having been institutionalised in Dublin since the 1830's) died... the estate passed to his brother, the Reverend Lucius Arthur.

Reverend Lucius was, however, actually living happily in a house at Matlock in Derbyshire, England... and never relocated to Ireland.

His son, Thomas Lucius Jervis Arthur (Desmond's Father) ultimately moved in instead... but, sadly, died shortly after his father (Rev. Lucius Arthur).

He left, as joint heirs to the Glenomera Estate, his two young sons: Charles William Augustus Arthur (c.1882-1937) and Desmond Phelps Pery Lucius Studdert Arthur (c.1884-1913).

His widow, Constance, raised the family at Glenomera until 1894.

After her remarriage, when Desmond was ten, they thereafter lived with her second husband, William Paumier Ball (c.1858-1902), in the salubrious surroundings of 71 Merrion Square in Dublin (the house which later became the home of Sybil Connolly and her couture studio).

Unfortunately, both William and his wife Constance died in 1902... leaving the two young men, who already had the reputation of being somewhat unruly and fearless, with extreme financial security... but without parental guidance.

Despite apparently not having been particularly close, both men joined the army together.

Desmond thereupon would develop a profound passion for flying.

Desmond's elder brother, Charles William Augustus Arthur, who was born on the 24th of September in 1882... became a Captain in the City of Limerick Artillery and the Royal Munster Fusiliers. After leaving the army, he emigrated to India in 1909.

Charles would have an adventurous, but troubled life... which would include a divorce in 1921; criminal charges and incarceration in Paris for 13 months for fraud in 1924; a failed expedition to hunt for pirate treasure on an island off the coast of Costa Rica in 1934... and eventually, bankruptcy in 1939, apparently after his death! He was married twice and had two sons: Charles Augustus Arthur (b. & d. 1905 - living less than one month), and Lucius Charles Algernon Arthur (c.1913-1992) both by his first wife, Violet Rose Roche-Kelly (c.1881-1927), the third daughter of John Joseph Roche-Kelly of Rockstown Castle and Islandmore in Limerick.

In 1930, he married Alice M.S. Aitken (alias Rodwell).

He supposedly died in Barbados or Trinidad in around 1937.

Desmond was schooled at Portora Royal Grammar School at Enniskillen, County Fermanagh (founded by the Royal Charter in 1608, by James I).

He was mesomorphic in build, approximately 5 feet 8 inch in height… and a keen sportsman, winning a number of prizes in motoring speed trials, among others.

After joining the army he soon became a Lieutenant in the Army Motor Reserve in 1908… thereafter joining the 5th Battalion of the Royal Munster Fusiliers (formerly the South Cork Light Infantry)… being promoted to Lieutenant on the 27th of May in 1911 (exactly two years to the day of his future death).

On the 29th of August in 1910, whilst in attendance at the inaugural aviation meeting of the 'Aero Club of Ireland' at Leopardstown Racecourse in Dún Laoghaire-Rathdown, Leinster (which was built by Captain George Quin (c.1842-1917) and modelled on Sandown Park Racecourse in England), he was introduced to Cecil Stanley Grace (c.1880-1910), a pioneer aviator (who went missing on a flight across the English Channel in 1910). It was this occasion which would fortify his desire for flying… and ultimately seal his fate.

On the 18th of June in 1912, Lt. Desmond L.S. Arthur attained his Royal Aero Club certificate (No. 233) upon the completion of his flying trials in a 'Bristol Prier monoplane' (designed for the Bristol and Colonial Aeroplane Company by Pierre Prier) in Brooklands Aviation Ground at Weybridge in Surrey, England.

P-1 No.46 Bristol Monoplane
(The first to be designed by Pierre Prier)

Now possessing his pilot's license... he soon transferred to the No.2 Squadron of the newly formed Royal Flying Corps.

No.1 Squadron had been formed as a balloon squadron for artillery observation.

In the first decade following the dawn of the twentieth century, the German empire was rapidly expanding... and would soon become a genuine threat to the security of the rest of Europe and, of course, Great Britain. They began to conclude that the North Sea should be regarded as their domain. Thus, in 1912, responding to the threat, the Government of Britain, under the instructions of the First Lord of the Admiralty, Winston Churchill, began planning the creation of a dozen 'Air Stations' to be operated by the, recently formed... 'Royal Flying Corps' (RFC).

In defence of the Royal Naval Fleet and their bases situated at Cromarty, Rosyth and Scapa Flow, it was logically decided that somewhere around the Scottish North-East coastal town of Montrose would provide the ideal locale for the first British Air Station.

On the 13th of February in 1913 (only nine years and fifty-eight days after the Wright brothers made their first powered flight), five aircraft belonging to the No.2 Squadron of the Royal Flying Corps (three Maurice Farman MF.11 Shorthorn and two B.E.2's), under the command of Major Charles James Burke DSO (Distinguished Service Order), took flight from RAE Farnborough (Royal Aircraft Establishment) in North-East Hampshire, heading northwards to Montrose. The 450 mile (720 km) journey took, ironically, a total of thirteen days to complete... having to be undertaken in carefully planned stages. On the 26th of February, the squadron landed about three miles (4.8 km) south of Montrose on the sloping field of a bare, windswept farm, known as 'Upper Dysart'. In spite of this place being less than ideal, it was still utilised as a temporary base (making it the first operational military airfield to be established in Great Britain). Being naturally dissatisfied with the site (plus only having flimsy wood and canvas hangars), Major Burke surveyed the surrounding areas for a more suitable location... eventually finding the desired terrain at 'Broomfield Farm', about one mile (1.6 km) north of Montrose... where the land was flat, being only thirty feet above sea level, in line with the prevailing wind and with good drainage due to the sandy soil. Being closer to the town and next to the railway line was also of great importance.

He was given authority to relocate the air station to Broomfield at the end of 1913. Royal Engineers (of the War Office's Directorate of Fortifications and Works) erected three hangars of 'Indian Army Shed' design (known as "Major Burke's sheds") on the site (pre-fabricated at Glasgow before being transported to Montrose and erected in December of 1913). No.2 Squadron moved to this base in the New Year of 1914.

Lieutenant Colonel Charles James Burke DSO (c.1882-1917) was a military aviation pioneer as well as an officer in the Royal Irish Regiment and the Royal Flying Corps (the youngest son of Michael Charles Christopher Burke of Ballinahone House, Armagh, Ireland). He was in command of No.2 Squadron… and subsequently the Second Wing (the First and Second Wings being created by necessity on the 29th of November in 1914). He began his British Army service in the 3rd Battalion of the Royal Dublin Fusiliers (being promoted to Lieutenant on the 24th of October in 1900), seeing active service in the Second Boer War. His service also included three years with the West African Frontier Force (WAFF). He was promoted to Captain in September of 1909. In 1910, Burke learned to fly in a Farman biplane whilst in France… shortly thereafter gaining his 'Aéro-Club de France' pilot's certificate.

Upon returning to England, he served in the 'School of Ballooning' (known as the 'Balloon Factory' prior to becoming the 'Royal Aircraft Factory') where he was involved in training and testing experiments with airships and balloons (established at Chatham in Kent in 1888). On the 13th of May in 1912, he became the commanding officer of the No. 2 Squadron of the Royal Flying Corps… and was promoted to Major.
During the next two years, he trained his squadron in aerial reconnaissance.

Although it was highly preferred that pilots be unmarried and weigh less than 11 stone 7 pounds… Charles Burke was not only 29 years old and married, but weighed well in excess of that which was desired (earning him the insensitive nickname of "Pregnant Percy"). Fortunately for him, his acceptance in the Royal Flying Corps was automatic due to him being among the few army pilots attached to the School of Ballooning (from which the Air Battalion grew).

In 1916 there was a severe shortage of officers, thus Lieutenant-Colonel Burke rejoined his old regiment (the Royal Irish Regiment). Tragically, he was killed in action on the 9th day of April in 1917, whilst commanding a battalion of the East Lancashire Regiment on the first day of the 'Battle of Arras'.

Lieutenant Colonel Charles James Burke DSO

In 1912, Charles Burke wrote his 29 maxims for flying:

1. Time in the air will alone make a pilot.
2. When training pilots, no machine should go out without knowing what it is to do, do it and it alone, then land.
3. When on the ground, everyone overrates their capacity for air-work.
4. No young pilot should be allowed out in "bumps" until he has done at least 15 hours piloting.
5. An aeroplane will live in the wind and a lifeboat in any sea, but they both want good and experienced men at the tiller.
6. Each smash means a certain amount of loss of the valuable assets: dash and keenness, though varying with individuals, the supply has its limits.
7. A pilot whose muscles are rigid when flying should do one of two things: (a) unstiffen (b) give up flying.
8. Napoleon Bonaparte said that in war the mental is to the physical as three to one. If he had known aviation, he would have put a nought after the three.
9. If the occupant of the passenger seat has no confidence in the pilot, there is probability of trouble. If it is the pilot who lacks confidence, the probability becomes a certainty.
10. In aviation, because a thing has been done without accident ten times is no guarantee that there will not be an accident on the eleventh.
11. The qualities mostly required by a pilot: confidence; by an observer: truth; by a rigger: reliability... and the first two are largely based on the last.
12. "Rumour is a lying jade." Aviation is full of rumours.
13. No pilots or anyone put over them will do any good if they listen to remarks actuated by jealousy.
14. Flying creates flying. If you see others up, the weather cannot be so bad as you imagined it was.
15. Divide pilots into classes. The weather will be fit for all of a class or none.
16. The amount of flying done does not depend on the weather but on the arrangements made to avail oneself of good weather.
17. Sufficient arrangements are seldom if ever made.
18. Aviation like arsenic can only be taken in small doses at first.
19. When things are going well, the man in charge can give play to his fears.
20. Nothing is ever as good or as bad as it seems.
21. Waiting about on an aerodrome has spoilt more pilots than everything else put together.
22. Strain can reduce the best of pilots by stages until it is just as dangerous for them to fly a machine as it is for a beginner.
23. Everyone who takes up flying becomes converted from disbelief into enthusiasm. Shortly after his conversion he may, or may not, kill himself.
24. Never regret having given a beginner too little flying at first, but always remember the time lost by want of arrangement.
25. If in doubt whether you should let beginners go up... "Don't".
26. A military flier is only becoming really valuable after six months, which is about the time that a civilian flier lasts as a star performer.

27 In aviation, all goes completely wrong or completely well. Neither should affect the man in charge as to what he intended to do.

28 If you know what you want, you can do your portion and get others to do theirs. Most people don't know what they want.

29 A Squadron Commander should want a good Squadron, and not be able to break records

Major C. J. Burke and No. 2 Squadron of the Royal Flying Corps
(Montrose, Scotland)

No. 2 Squadron of the Royal Flying Corps
(Montrose, Scotland)

Knights of the Air
(Montrose, Scotland)

In June of 1914, the Royal Flying Corps consisted of five aircraft squadrons: No.2, 3, 4, 5 and 6.

No.1 Squadron was in the process of converting from balloons, while No.7 was still being formed.

Upon the outbreak of World War One on the 4th of August in 1914, the Military Wing of the RFC was comprised of 147 officers and 1,097 men with 179 aircraft.

Amid the war… the RFC underwent expeditious augmentation… and by the end of 1916, had 46,000 personnel and 2,712 aircraft in 64 operational and 33 reserve squadrons.

A year later there were 10,938 aircraft in 115 operational and 109 training squadrons.

The flying training school, as with many others, experienced frequent crashes as it built up a force of skilled pilots.

There was no handbook telling the first instructors what methods they were to use in teaching their cadets wartime manoeuvres in an aircraft.

Although an instructor could be capable of teaching his students with profound insight, he was often so stressed and overworked that his expertise could be drastically impaired.

Even accomplished pilots were always at risk due to the inherent dangers of flying.

Prelude to Flight

Desmond Arthur was only 29 years, 1 month and 26 days old when he was tragically killed.

Around seven o'clock in the morning of the 27th of May in 1913... he took off from the temporary No.2 Squadron airfield at Upper Dysart Farm for a training flight above Lunan Bay in his Renault 70 horsepower (Royal Aircraft Factory) B.E.2c (Blériot Experimental) biplane No.205 (designed by Captain Sir Geoffrey de Havilland (c.1882-1965) and Lieutenant Edward Teshmaker Busk (c.1886-1914).

Lt. Arthur's B.E.2c Biplane No.205
(Upper Dysart Farm Airfield, Scotland)

About forty minutes later... whilst flying over Montrose, upon beginning his decent at approximately two thousand five hundred feet, the upper right wing collapsed and broke off without warning due to a broken spar, which had hitherto remained unseen... as it had been concealed under the plane's fabric. The biplane subsequently went into a violent spin as it hurtled towards the ground. It remains unclear whether Lt. Arthur chose to jump from the cockpit or was thrown out, possibly due to his seatbelt snapping... but nevertheless, he fell over two thousand feet to an instant death.

The foreman of the Lunan House estate farm, belonging to Captain Hew Francis Blair-Imrie CMG (c.1873-1942), reported seeing the biplane shortly before hearing a crashing sound which accompanied the plane's brutal descent. Disturbingly, he also reported seeing a body plummeting to the earth. He described the person as falling perfectly straight and silently… with the arms held directly above the head. He fell for approximately 13 seconds.

Medical assistance was quickly summoned to the scene. Lt. Arthur's shattered body was found 156 yards away from the mangled wreckage of his biplane which had crashed near the Lunan Bay railway station (which was opened on the 1st of May in 1883 by the North British, Arbroath and Montrose Railway).

Wreckage of Lt. Arthur's B.E.2c Biplane No.205
(Near Lunan, Scotland)

Curiously, 'The Aeroplane' magazine stated in an article that Lt. Arthur had taken the plane up for a preliminary test flight… and that it was "flying splendidly". The initial investigation into the incident was conducted by the Royal Aero Club (on the 2nd and 10th of June) which pronounced that an inadequate repair to a spar on the wing was the cause of the crash.

It was stated that the plane had been built in June of 1912 and rebuilt again in August. There was a definite suspicion that accidental damage to the machine had been deliberately covered up by an 'unknown' mechanic at Farnborough, but not that this had been done maliciously. There was no record made of the repair. The following report was issued on the 21st of June in 1913: "The Committee is of the opinion that the primary cause of the accident was the failure of the faulty joint in the repair to the rear main spar."

A government inquiry commenced on the 11th of July in 1913. In 1914, William Joynson-Hicks MP, 1st Viscount Brentford (c.1865-1932) complained of a 'whitewash' of the matter… and that Colonel John Edward Bernard Seely, 1st Baron Mottistone (c.1868-1947) 'Secretary of State for War'… refused to admit to the faulty repair. Further criticism came from another member in 1916… British aviator, inventor and publisher, Noel Pemberton Billing (c. 1865-1932), head of 'Pemberton Billing Limited' aircraft manufacturers, who called for a judicial enquiry into the military and naval air services. He stated: "certain officers had been murdered rather than killed by the carelessness, incompetence or ignorance of their senior officers or of the technical side of those two services."

William Joynson-Hicks MP   Noel Pemberton Billing

The government only responded by setting up their own enquiry on the 3rd of August in 1916.

This Interim Report concluded that pilot error and dangerous flying had caused Lt. Arthur's death; something that was strongly disputed by contemporary pilots in the Royal Flying Corps… where rumours abounded. Although the Final Report was dated on the 17th of November in 1916, it did not appear until Christmas, but it went some way at least towards exonerating Lt. Arthur… and clearing his name.

Lt. Arthur's Death Registration

Lt. Desmond Arthur was buried with full military honours.

Lt. Arthur's Funeral Procession
(Montrose, Scotland)

The funeral procession made its way through the town of Montrose and was followed by a memorial service in St. Mary's and St. Peter's Episcopal Church on Panmure Street… thereafter it carried onward to Desmond's final resting place in Sleepyhillock Cemetery.

St. Mary's and St. Peter's Episcopal Church
(Montrose, Scotland)

Lt. Arthur's Grave
in
Sleepyhillock Cemetery
(Montrose, Scotland)
2020

Upon the examination of Lt. Arthur's broken body... a locket was retrieved from the breast pocket of his uniform... inside which, a miniature portrait of a young woman was enclosed... the glass having been cracked by the impact. Her name was Constance Winsome Ropner (affectionately called "wis").

Constance Winsome Ropner
(c.1899-1988)

Lt. Arthur had known the Ropner family for at least a decade prior to his death.

When residing at the County Durham seaside resort of Seaton Carew in North East England, he had formed a warm and close friendship with the young girl's parents… a successful Hartlepool shipowner, William Robert Ropner (c.1864-1947) and his wife, Sarah Woollacott Cory (c.1868-1948). William Ropner's father was Sir (Emil Hugo Oscar) "Robert" Ropner, 1st Baronet (c.1838-1924). He was a German-British shipbuilder, shipowner and Conservative Member of Parliament… born 'Röpner' (pronounced 'Roopner') at Magdeburg in the Kingdom of Prussia, the son of Johann Heinrich Röpner and Johanne Christiane Emilie Bessel.

Over the years Lt. Arthur spent many holidays with them at their home in Ambleside House on Elwick Road in West Hartlepool, Durham.

As young Constance Winsome grew… so did love between she and Desmond. Despite the fifteen year age difference… a future marriage seemed destined. Proprieties were, of course, always observed and they were never alone together.

She was fourteen when Lt. Arthur departed Ambleside House for the final time. Two weeks later, he was dead.

The overwhelming grief experienced by all concerned can only be imagined.

Ambleside House
(West Hartlepool, Durham, England)

When Lt. Arthur's will was read at Dublin on the 9th of June in 1913, it was revealed that he had left most of his wealth (being £9,569) to Miss Constance Winsome Ropner, his intended future bride.

The sum of £1,000 was bequeathed to his elder brother Charles, subject to the agreement of Miss Ropner. The will was contested by Charles Arthur… but upheld by Justice William Kenny (c.1846-1921) at the Irish High Court in 1914. In order to fulfil the bequest, the Glenomera estate had to be sold (The Ropner family were obviously wealthy, so why they fought Charles W. A. Arthur in court to uphold Lt. Arthur's will can only be speculated upon… and why Lt. Arthur basically snubbed his brother, also remains to be seen. Charles was also cut out of his own mother's will… perhaps because he was somewhat of a rogue… as well as having frivolously spent all of his share of the money his father had bequeathed to him. He did pay for his brother's monument at Sleepyhillock Cemetery however).

Constance Winsome Ropner would go on to eventually marry the war hero, Major George Talbot Willcox RFC in October of 1922, whom she would ultimately outlive by a further twenty years. She died aged 89.

She never forgot Desmond Arthur, her 'first love'… and would name her firstborn son after him.

Somewhere in Time

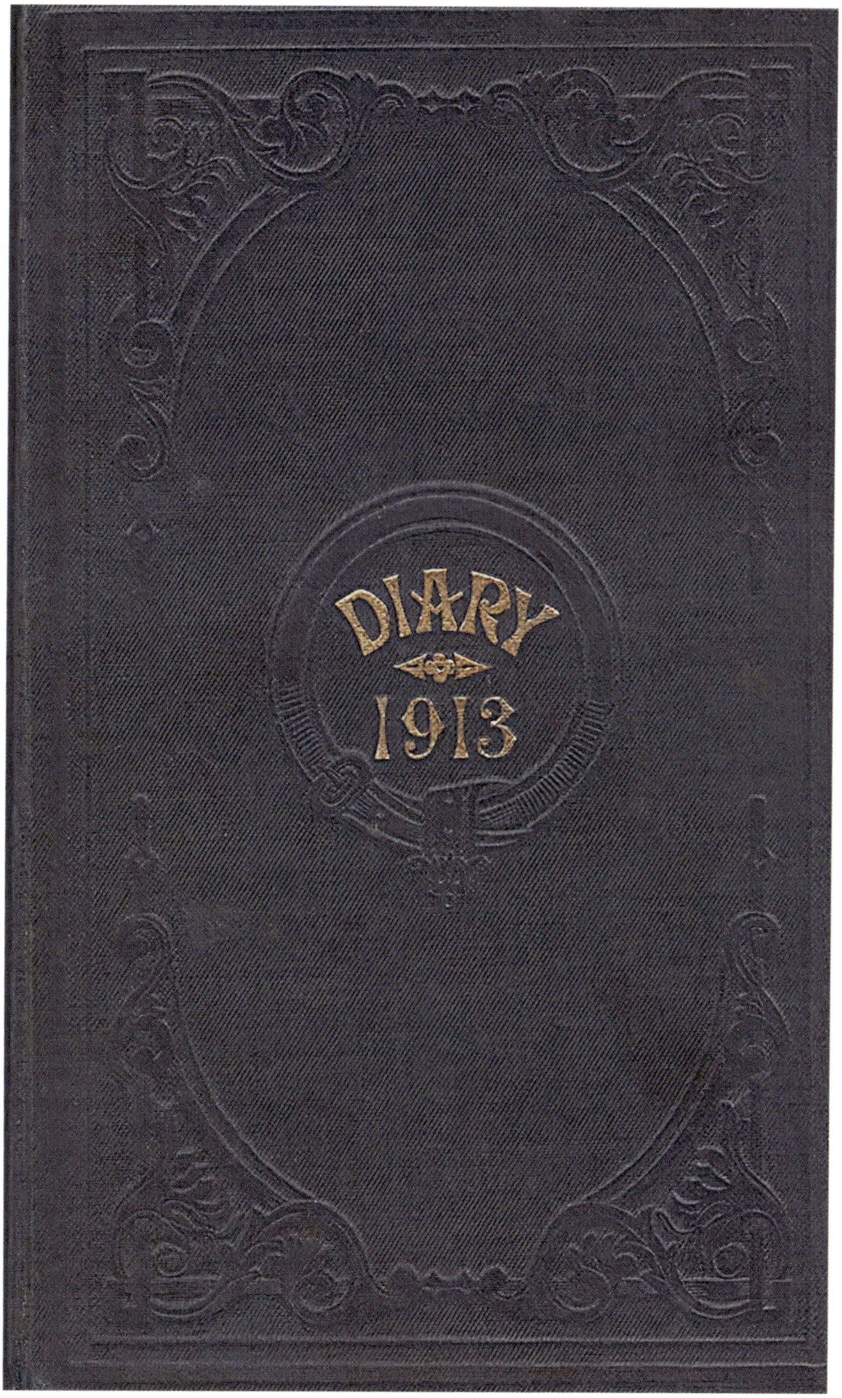

Lt. Arthur's Diary

The alleged haunting of 'Montrose Air Station' did not happen until about three years after Lt. Arthur's death.

It was during 1916 that reports of an unknown airman began to surface at Montrose.

Lt. Arthur had never actually visited the area at any point whilst he was alive.

One prominent witness was a senior flying instructor named Major Cyril Edgar Foggin (c.1891-1918) who saw the ghost on a number of occasions.

One evening when he was making his way to the mess, he saw a figure going the same way... and then vanish when it reached the door. He put the sighting down to overwork and did not initially communicate it for fear he would jeopardise his position.

The paranormal researcher and author, Peter Underwood, wrote that Major Foggin witnessed the ghost FIVE times during that autumn... and that the figure was also witnessed by the station commander and several witnesses who were flying instructors.

One of the latter woke at night to see a uniformed man sitting in a chair in his room, but when he challenged it, the person vanished.

The ghost made one last appearance on Christmas Eve in 1916... and then disappeared.

What firmly re-established Lt. Desmond Arthur as the 'Montrose ghost' was an article by Sir Peter Masefield (the aviation journalist and former chairman of the British Airports Authority) in 'Flight International' in December of 1972 (by which time RAF Montrose had closed).

In the article, Masefield repeated the original story of Lt. Arthur's death and the subsequent appearance of his spirit at Montrose with an important new twist in the tale.

As Masefield was leaving Dalcross (Inverness airport), he was approached by a man who asked for a lift in the rear seat of his 'de Havilland Canada DHC-1 Chipmunk' aircraft... so he took off with a passenger. As the Chipmunk approached Montrose, Masefield was astonished to encounter an ancient B.E2 biplane flying over the old airfield... and to his horror... he saw its wing collapse and the pilot fall from the cockpit. There was a cry from his passenger but when Masefield turned round, there was nobody there!

Badly shaken, Masefield landed at Montrose, took on petrol and then continued his flight to Brooklands Airfield.

When he went to write up his logbook he saw that the date was the 27th of May (1963)... exactly 50 years since Desmond Arthur's fatal accident.

He had witnessed a re-enactment of the tragedy!

Masefield stated: "is there a 'Montrose ghost'... and is it Desmond Arthur? There are certainly recent sightings of apparitions of men in flying dress which defy rational explanation but we should remember that hundreds of men were killed at Montrose over two World Wars. Circumstances point to the existence, if that is the right term, of many ghosts. As far as Lt. Arthur is concerned, we should go back to the original story.

He returned briefly for a purpose... and once he was cleared of the blame for the accident... he departed. We should now let him rest in peace!"

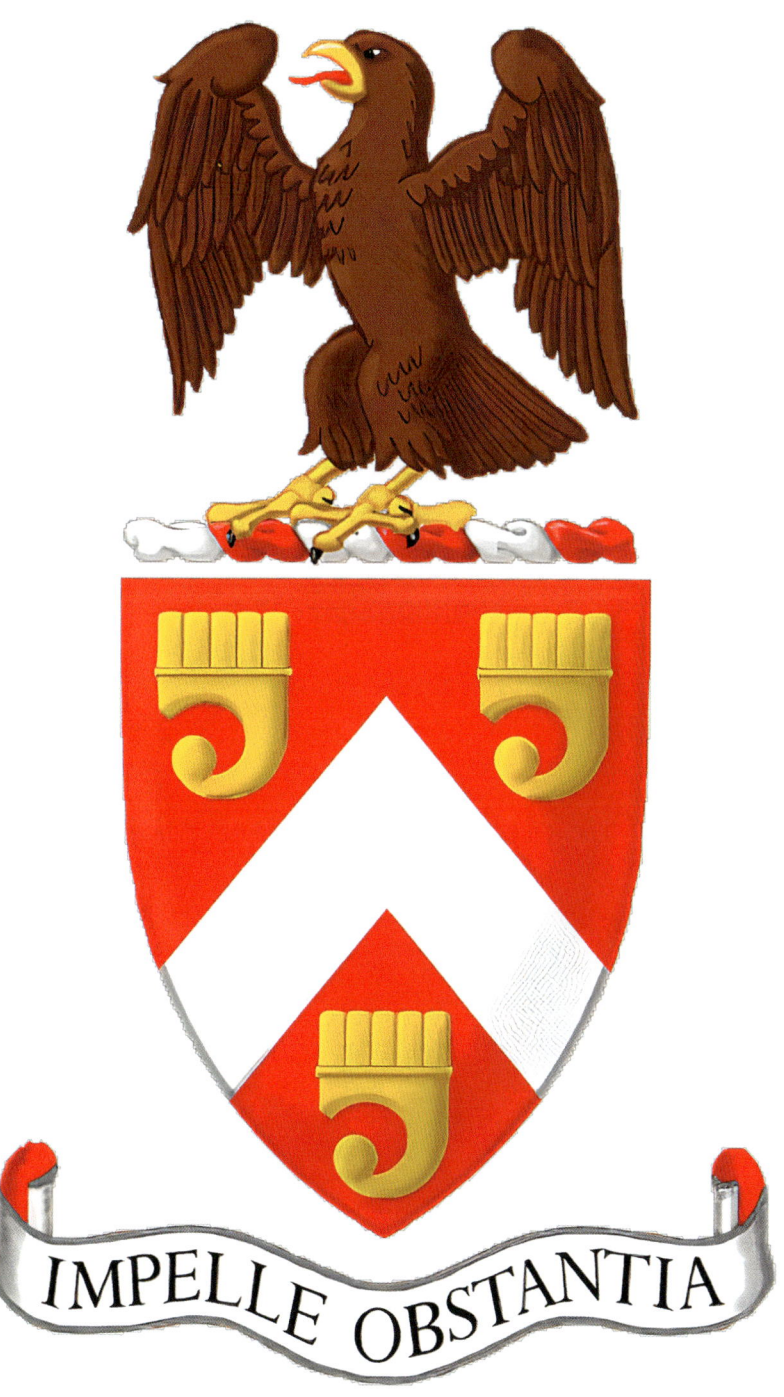

The Arthur Family Crest

MONTROSE AIR STATION
WORLD WAR ONE
ROLL OF HONOUR

I

Arthur. D.L.S. Lieutenant
27/05/1913
Royal Flying Corps, Montrose
Sleepyhillock Cemetery

Alger. G.C. 2nd-Lieutenant
07/06/1917
Royal Flying Corps, Montrose
Sleepyhillock Cemetery

Arthur. E.P. Lieutenant
24/12/1917
Australian Flying Corps, Montrose
Sleepyhillock Cemetery

Arthur. L.F. 2nd-Lieutenant
28/03/1918
Royal Flying Corps, Montrose
Sleepyhillock Cemetery

Burton. E.W. Lieutenant
04/04/1918
Australian Flying Corps, Montrose
Sleepyhillock Cemetery

II

Cangiamila. J. 2nd-Lieutenant
12/08/1918
Royal Air Force, Montrose
Sleepyhillock Cemetery

Churchill. F.D. 2nd-Lieutenant,
08/05/1918
Royal Air Force, Montrose
Sleepyhillock Cemetery

Craik. A. Member
03/11/1918
Woman's Royal Air Force, Montrose
Sleepyhillock Cemetery

Findlay. L. Captain
14/06/1917
Royal Flying Corps, Montrose
Sleepyhillock Cemetery

Foot. D.V. 2nd-Lieutenant
04/05/1917
Royal Flying Corps, Montrose
Bo'ness Cemetery

III

Frederick. L.M. 2nd-Lieutenant
08/07/1918
Royal Air Force, Montrose
Sleepyhillock Cemetery

Gaster. P.S. 2nd-Lieutenant
21/04/1918
Royal Air Force, London
Camberwell Old Cemetery

Grayham. W.J.K. 2nd-Lieutenant
17/05/1918
Royal Air Force, Montrose
Sleepyhillock Cemetery

Grimshaw. G.H. 2nd-Lieutenant
08/07/1918
Royal Air Force
Manchester Macclesfield Cemetery

Hall. J.H. Lieutenant
25/08/1918
Royal Air Force
Manchester Bury Cemetery

IV

Henderson. W.D. Flight Cadet
28/11/1918
Royal Air Force
Gloucester Old Cemetery

Lewis. F.A. 2nd-Lieutenant
28/03/1918
Royal Air Force, Montrose
Sleepyhillock Cemetery

Marriott. G. 2nd-Lieutenant
19/07/1918
Royal Air Force
Sunninghill St. Michael Churchyard

McLaren. F.W.S. 2nd-Lieutenant
30/08/1918
Royal Flying Corps
Surrey Busbridge Churchyard

Middleton. G.N. 2nd-Lieutenant
22/02/1918
Royal Flying Corps, Montrose
Sleepyhillock Cemetery

V

Moore. J.A. 2nd-Lieutenant
11/11/1917
Royal Flying Corps, Montrose
Sleepyhillock Cemetery

Mott. A.E.P. Lieutenant
24/12/1917
Australian Flying Corps, Montrose
Sleepyhillock Cemetery

Morrison. J.S. 2nd-Lieutenant
13/10/1916
Royal Flying Corps, Montrose
Sleepyhillock Cemetery

Percival. H.K. Flight Cadet
23/09/1918
Royal Air Force, Montrose
Sleepyhillock Cemetery

Preston. M.E. 2nd-Lieutenant
23/09/1918
Royal Air Force, Montrose
Sleepyhillock Cemetery

VI

Reid. C.D. NCO Cadet
05/09/1918
Royal Air Force
Glasgow Craigton Cemetery

Roach. D.J. 2nd-Lieutenant
23/05/1918
Royal Air Force, Montrose
Sleepyhillock Cemetery

Stevenson. J. 2nd-Lieutenant
01/05/1917
Royal Flying Corps
Orkney Evie Cemetery

Thompson. W.C. Lieutenant
16/10/1917
Royal Flying Corps, Montrose
Sleepyhillock Cemetery

Taylor-Loban. G. Captain
07/06/1917
Royal Flying Corps, Montrose
Sleepyhillock Cemetery

VII

Walker. R.P. 2nd-Lieutenant
22/05/1918
Royal Air Force, Stirling
Alloa (Sunnyside) Cemetery

William. F. 2nd-Lieutenant,
16/11/1916
Royal Flying Corps, Montrose
Sleepyhillock Cemetery

William. H. Corporal
16/09/1915
Royal Flying Corps, Montrose
Sleepyhillock Cemetery

Wilson. A.C. Corporal
25/08/1916
Royal Flying Corps, Montrose
Sleepyhillock Cemetery

... AND THE MANY OTHERS

"They shall grow not old, as we that are left grow old:
Age shall not weary them, nor the years condemn.
At the going down of the sun and in the morning,
We will remember them."

Robert Laurence Binyon
English poet, dramatist and art scholar
1869 ~ 1943

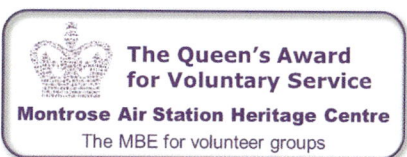

Please consider a donation and share our story.
All donations will be greatly appreciated and go directly to preserving our museum.
Tel. 01674 678222

I stood by the edge of a cloud-mantled ledge,
Looking down upon eagles in flight.
Sunlight reflections of gold on their backs
Filled my eyes with diaphanous light.

I stood above freedom; I looked upon God;
I saw my own Soul without chains.
I knew in my Heart that we're all, simply, One…
And that Love, will be all that remains.

BDG

Further reading :

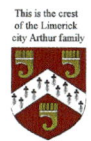  

Acknowledgements

I GRATEFULLY ACKNOWLEDGE THE HELP AND GUIDANCE OF
ALL THOSE WHO DIRECTLY OR INDIRECTLY ASSISTED IN THIS ENDEAVOUR…
BUT PARTICULARLY THE FOLLOWING :

MONTROSE AIR STATION HERITAGE CENTRE AND ITS VOLUNTEERS;
STUART ARCHIBALD (MASHC CHAIRMAN);
HELEN FRANCES GRAHAM;
DENNIS ADNE GRAHAM;
HANNAH HELENA MARGARET GRAHAM;
JONATHAN CHRISTOPHER JAMES GRAHAM;
PETER BAKER;
JOHN MOLLOY;
MICHAEL KELLY;
PAUL KELLY;
NICHOLAS ARTHUR;
PAUL WILLCOX;
DR. DAN PATON;
SIR PETER MASEFIELD;
JASON SALKEY;
JOHN TAMS
AND
THE MONTROSE LIBRARY

Bibliography

I. Burke's Landed Gentry of Ireland, 1912.

II. Joynson-Hicks, William, (ed) Safety of Army Aeroplanes, 1914.

III. Montrose Air Station Heritage Centre.

IV. The National Archives, Kew.

V. PHPBB Library Forum.

VI. Royal Air Force Museum, London.

VII. Raleigh, Walter, (ed) The History of the War in the Air, 1922.

VIII. Turner, Charles Cyril, (ed) Government and Flying, 1927.

IX. Underwood, Peter, (ed) The Gazetteer of Scottish Ghosts, London, 1974.

About the Author

Barry Dominic Graham was born in the Benedictine Crerar Hospital near the Cree Nation Reserve in Winnipegosis, Manitoba, Canada.

He is of Scots/Irish ancestry.

He grew up in Glasgow, Scotland where he attended St Brendan's Primary School, Yoker; Corpus Christi Primary School, Knightswood; and St Thomas Aquinas Secondary School, Jordanhill (as did some notable others, such as the actor, James McAvoy; singer, Justin Osuji and soccer player, Tosh McKinlay).

Over the years he has lived in Canada in several British Columbian locations, namely Hope, Abbotsford, and Kelowna, as well as Prince Albert in Saskatchewan.

His son, Jonathan, lives and works in British Columbia, Canada.

Barry now resides in Montrose, with his wife Helen Frances and daughter Hannah Helena.

He is an author, poet, composer and historical researcher.

By the same author:

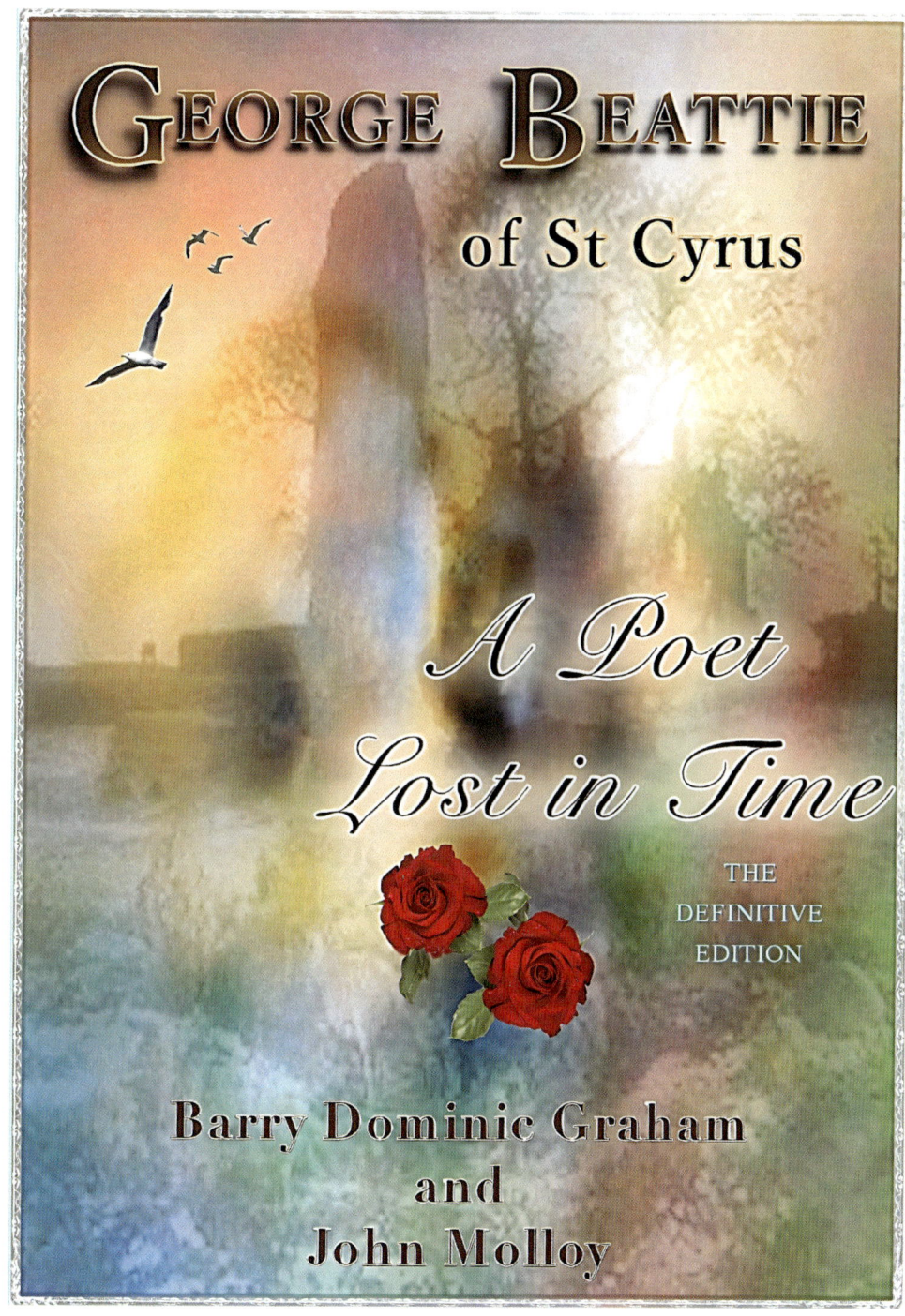

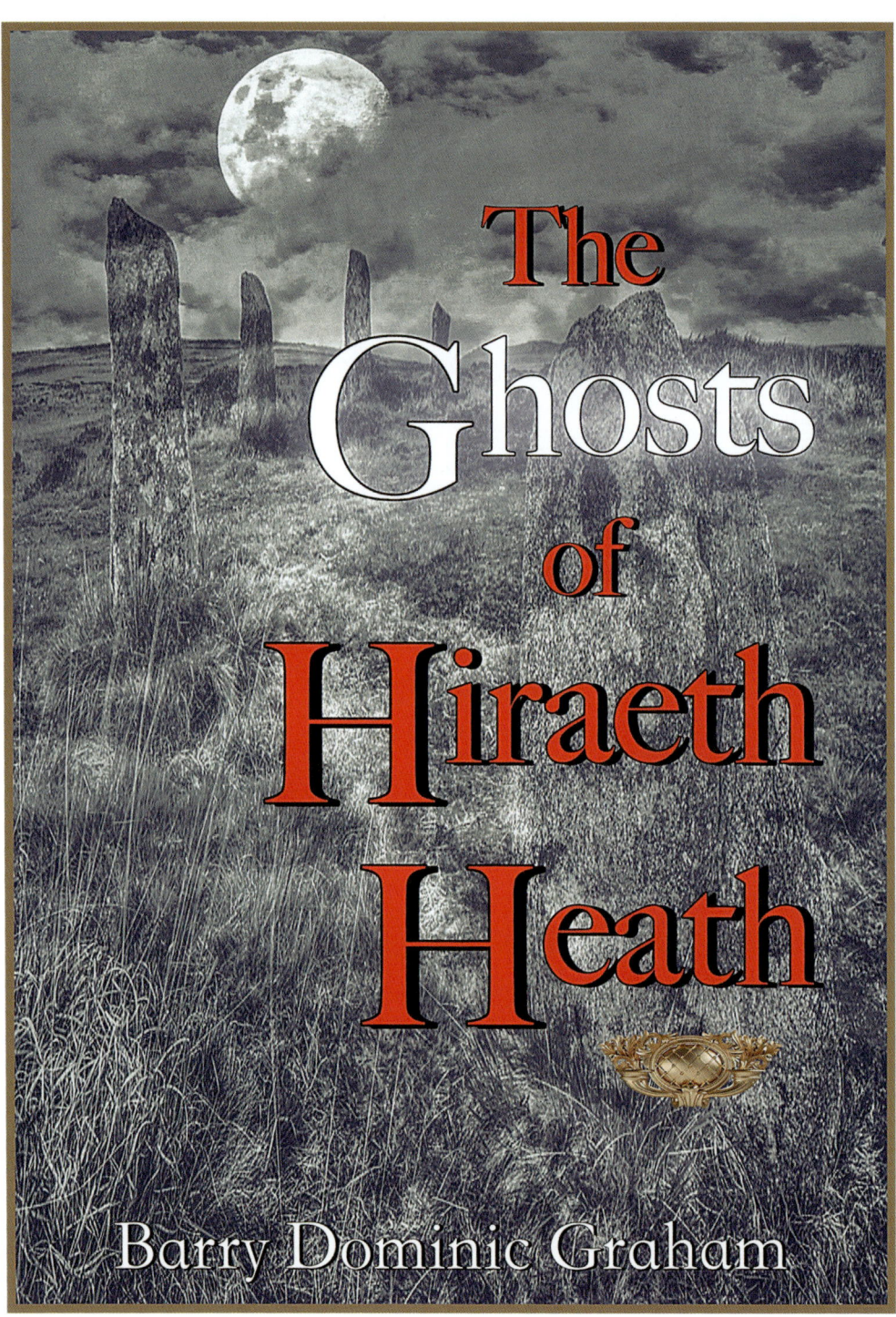

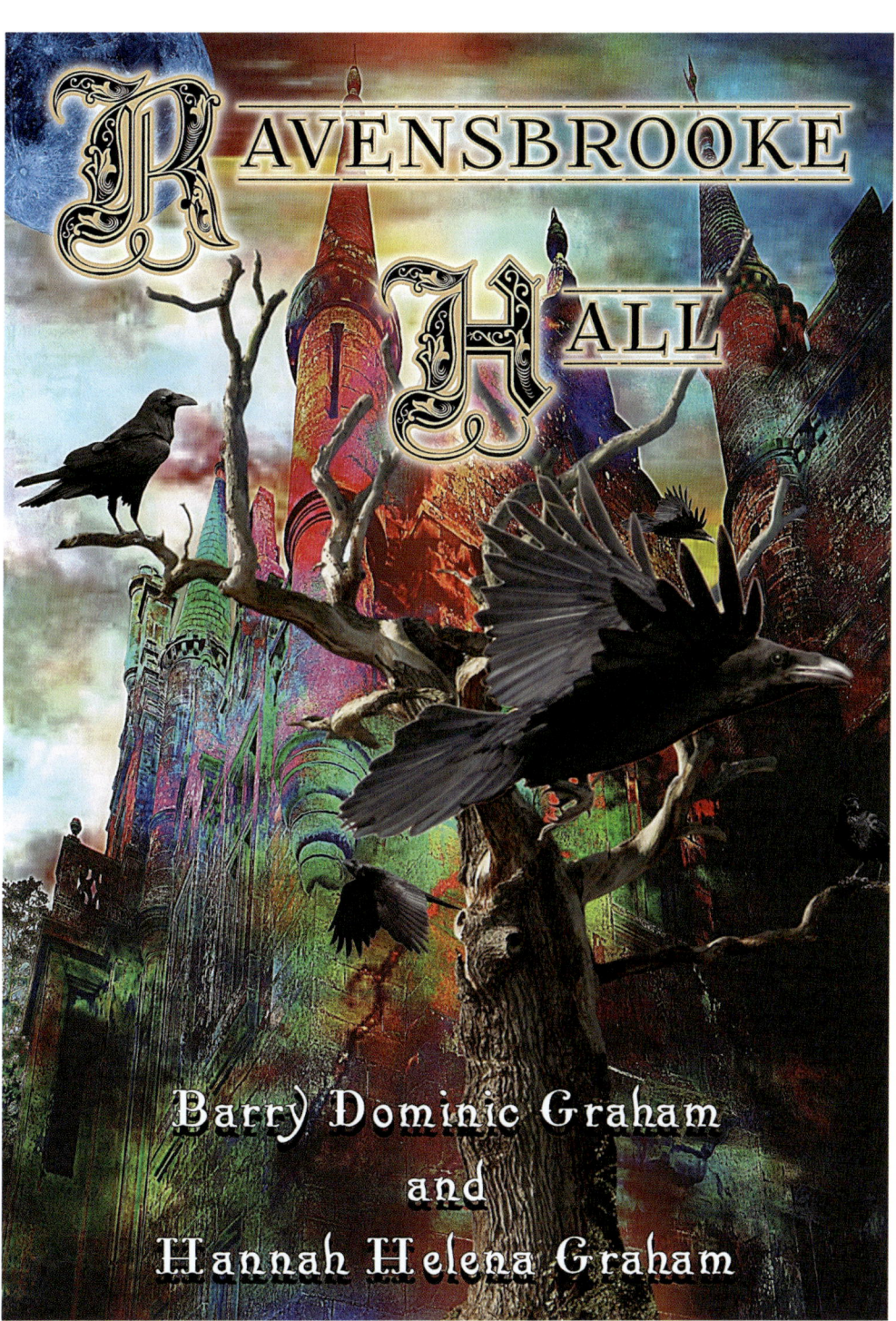

Printed in Great Britain
by Amazon